The Long Walk HOME

CONTENTS

Chapter One	5
Chapter Two	15
Chapter Three	23
Chapter Four	29
Chapter Five	37
Chapter Six	43
Chapter Seven	51
Chapter Eight	59
Chapter Nine	67
Chapter Ten	77

CHAPTER ONE

Brad had always found that if he concentrated really hard on something, whatever it was that was hurting him inside would go away. But it didn't seem to work anymore. It hadn't worked very well ever since Dad left.

The trouble was, Brad decided, there was more than one thing hurting him. There were many. It was just like trying to push inflatable toys underwater in a pool. Just when he managed to push one problem under a more pleasant thought, another problem would pop up.

Now, his mother, her eyes happy and shining, was going out with a man to celebrate selling their house. He didn't know which problem was worse – the fact that his mother was going out with someone as if he were a boyfriend, or their house being sold.

Brad stared at Gary Hebbleton for a moment. Gary hadn't been a neighbor for long, but he had become a comfortable family friend. Brad had enjoyed helping him replace faucet washers or fix the fence. He had become used to him stopping over now and again for coffee on weekends. Gary Hebbleton seemed like a kind and friendly man.

But that didn't mean he should be taking Brad's mother out. That didn't mean he should be acting as though it were a wonderful thing that they had sold their house – the place where Brad and Mom and Dad belonged.

"We're going out to Alfredo's tonight for dinner," his mother was saying happily. Gary Hebbleton was smiling.

"Why are you celebrating selling our house?" Brad yelled. Even he was surprised at how loudly his voice came out. It was almost like his thoughts were exploding from his head. "It's our house! No one has any right to live here but us!"

Then he raced out of the kitchen and down through the backyard to the big, old tree in the corner. He climbed high up into its branches and pretended not to hear when his mother came out, calling his name.

She soon went back inside. Instead of feeling glad that she didn't know where he was, Brad was angry that she hadn't bothered to look for him for any longer. "Nobody cares about me." He wrenched a piece of bark from the trunk, flung it to the ground, and watched it break into pieces.

For nearly an hour, he stayed up in the tree. It was only the smell of chicken wafting over the fence from the Baxters' house next door that made him come inside.

"Brad, moving won't be so bad," his mother said as she fixed his dinner. "You'll have a new room and we'll paint it any color you want."

Brad looked at his mother. "Black," he said. "I want it to be totally black — all of it."

His mother turned the chops before she said, "Don't be silly, Brad. Black wouldn't look good at all. Besides, every speck of dust would show."

"But you said I could paint it whatever color I wanted."

His mother sighed heavily. "We'll talk about it another time."

"I'll still want it to be black."

Dad had been angry about Mom wanting to sell the house. He had called, and Brad had heard them arguing. Well, he'd heard Mom talking – until he hid under his blankets.

There had always seemed like there was a small chance Dad would come back if they were in their own house. But when Brad had begged that they stay where they were, his mother had said firmly, "I'm starting over. We're not going away from your friends or your school, but there is no way I'm staying in this house."

She had put the house on the market, and Brad had been secretly pleased that it stayed unsold for eight months.

That is, until today, Brad thought as he watched his mom cook.

"You and John Baxter can watch that movie on TV while he's staying with you tonight," Brad's mother said, giving him a hug. "Then off to bed."

Lying in bed after the movie, Brad thought about lying in bed in another house. He didn't want another house or another room – no matter what color it was. He wanted this room with the stain on the carpet where he'd spilled the cocoa, and the small high windows with the bubbly glass in which he could see animal shapes if he stared at them from his bed. He wanted his room with the striped curtains he had chosen, and the closet door that squeaked no matter how often it was oiled.

Then Brad remembered the bike he wanted. His mother had said, "When the house is sold, we'll know what our money situation is. Then we can think about things like a mountain bike."

Brad heard his mother arrive home. Well, his mother and Gary Hebbleton. He heard them paying John for watching him, and he heard the door shutting. Brad wanted to yell, "Mommaaa!" like he used to when he was little, but it seemed like a stupid thing to do now that he was eleven.

Instead, he got out of bed and made his way to the partly open door to the living room. He could see his mother sitting on the couch, talking as if she would never stop, and Gary Hebbleton listening to her as if he had never heard anyone talk before. Sometimes they both laughed.

He suddenly pushed the door open.

"Brad! You should be sound asleep."

"I want to talk to you."

"Is it important?" she asked.

"Yes, it is."

"Go ahead," Gary Hebbleton laughed. "You're needed. I'll be here when you get back."

Brad scowled at him, but Gary was too busy laughing to notice.

"What's so important that you have to interrupt me at this hour?" his mother demanded.

"I want a bike." Brad jumped onto his bed and wriggled under the covers.

"You've got a..."

"No, I want a mountain bike. You said when the house was sold that I could have my own mountain bike."

"I said we would think about it. First we have to see how much another house will cost."

"Something else always comes first. I'm never first. No one ever thinks about me. Nobody asks what I think about anything," Brad groaned.

"Brad!"

"I want to stay in our house. You shouldn't have sold it!"

"We'll talk about this in the morning, Brad." His mother's voice was tight, and then it softened a little. "Things won't seem so bad in the morning. Now, go to sleep, Brad."

"No, I don't want to," he mumbled to himself, and then in a louder voice he called out, "I'm getting a drink of water."

She was back at his doorway before he could lift his head from the pillow. Her voice was sharp. "Stay right there! I have a guest, and I don't want to be interrupted again!"

The door to the living room clicked shut.

Gary Hebbleton wasn't a guest, thought Brad. He was her date. His mother had gone on a date. It wasn't fair. He just wanted his father back home. He didn't want to move, either. And he wanted someone to care about what he thought.

Brad sat up in bed. "Nothing is the same anymore. Well, I'm not moving. I'm going to run away. I'm going to run away to Longford."

CHAPTER TWO

Brad had often dreamed about running away, and now he was going to do it. Everyone would be sorry they hadn't cared enough to listen to him.

"Brad, will you hurry up?" His mother had finished her breakfast and was rushing to get ready for work. She hadn't mentioned the mountain bike even though she'd said they would talk about it in the morning."

"Don't forget to lock up, Brad," she said as she rushed out the door.

"She didn't even say bye," muttered Brad. He forced himself to eat another slice of toast as fuel for his journey. "I bet she'll wish she had."

In the kitchen, he combed the cupboards for food he could carry easily. Eventually, he began to put the food he thought he might need on the counter.

He found a loaf of bread, some margarine and mustard, four packages of powdered fruit juice, six slices of bacon, four slices of ham, two cans of sardines, six apples, four packages of dried soup, half a bag of rice, and one box of raisins. He added half a dozen eggs even though they'd be hard to carry, because they would taste good with bacon.

In the big garage cupboard he found the camping gear. He dusted off a frying pan and a small pot, found a plastic mug, two plates, and a knife, fork, and spoon.

Worried about space, he wedged a thin sleeping bag into his school backpack. He packed the food on top, juggling the packages and cans until they fit snuggly.

He remembered how he'd protested that his pack was too big when his mother had bought it for him last year. She had told him to stop grumbling. "It will last you through college when you have piles of books to carry."

He wasn't grumbling now.

He added a parka, socks, a sweater, two T-shirts, some more shorts, and some underwear.

Time. He had to watch the time so he could catch the first bus to Longford. Bus... money... He emptied a small stack of coins from his bank and a couple of dollars from his drawer.

Then the doorbell rang. Brad froze. He heard the door opening and footsteps coming in. His best friend called, "It's just Turtle. Are you still here, Brad?"

Brad dived out of the doorway and met Turtle Taylor in the hall. "I'm running a little late, Turtle. You go on ahead."

"It's OK. I'm early. That's why I stopped by."

"Just go, Turtle. I might make you late."

"It doesn't matter." Turtle shrugged his shoulders and grinned his lazy grin. "What do you have to do? I'll help."

"No, no. I won't be long. Can you check that the front door's locked?"

Brad was out of time. He wouldn't be able to check his packing. His mind whirled as he tried to remember whether he had everything. He tightened the straps on his pack and wished he could tell Turtle what he was doing. He wished he could have Turtle come with him. But the problem wasn't Turtle's.

He had planned on going straight to the bus station, but now that Turtle was here, he didn't see how he could avoid going to school, or at least pretending to go to school before he sneaked off. Well, he wasn't taking his bike. He grabbed his cap from the peg, calling to Turtle as he went out the door.

"My bike has a flat tire," he lied and jogged beside his friend, who pedaled in the lowest gear. Turtle had gotten his mountain bike a year ago.

"Hey, what a huge pack," Turtle said suddenly. "What's in it?"

"Nothing much. Just some stuff."

"Come on, what's in it?" Turtle slowed to get behind Brad, and he poked at the bulging pack.

"Leave it alone!" Brad said sharply.

There was silence for half a block. Brad knew that Turtle didn't understand why Brad was angry with him. Eventually he said, "My mother won't let me get a mountain bike."

"You'll get one someday," said Turtle. "I think Colin Fowler's giving up his after-school job. You could try to get that."

They turned in at the school gate. "Go ahead and put your bike in the bike rack. I'll see you later in class," said Brad.

"Hey!" Puzzled, Turtle looked behind him as Brad headed off across the school grounds. "Hey, we're pretty late. We better go straight to class."

Brad suddenly felt bad about tricking his best friend. He shouldn't lie to him. He took a few steps back. "Turtle, don't say anything. Please don't say anything. I'm not going to class today. I'm going to Longford."

Turtle stared at him, not understanding what Brad was talking about.

"You know – to the forest at Longford where there's that hut where I stayed with Dad."

"What do you mean?" asked Turtle. "What for?"

"Don't say you came to school with me. Pretend you didn't see me." Brad was wishing now that he hadn't told Turtle. There was no way his friend could understand. "I'm running away. Nobody cares, so I'm running away."

Then he ran as fast as the weight of his pack would let him, across the tennis courts, out the gate, and down the road. He didn't look back once, and that was partly because he could feel tears stinging his eyes. Turtle's voice yelled behind him, "Hey, I care, Brad! I care!"

CHAPTER THREE

Hiking along the sun-dappled path, Brad tried to keep a steady pace. Although the sun was filtered by the overhanging foliage, the day was warm.

After an hour, Brad was pleased to turn off the path, find a mossy seat by the river, and take off his pack. He removed his shoes and socks, scrunching up his toes in delight when the cold water closed over his dangling feet. Brad lay back on the mossy bank.

Overhead the sky was summer blue, its edges fringed with high branches. In front of him ran the river, and beyond it was a great expanse of forest that seemed to go on forever.

It had been so easy. The owner of the sporting goods store didn't act surprised that Brad was in his store at nine o'clock in the morning, buying dehydrated food from the camping section.

His confidence high, Brad went into the stationery store next door. On a postcard he wrote, "You don't need to worry about me. I am fine." By the time he mailed it to his mother, he needed to run to catch the bus.

As he took Brad's ticket, the bus driver hardly gave him a second glance. Brad's pounding heart stopped racing, and he settled into a seat. His cap was stuck rather clammily to his head, but he left it on. There was no point in advertising the fact that he had mousy hair, gray eyes, and freckles.

Brad got off the bus at Longford, walked quickly through the rest of the town, and went down a country road to the forest turnoff. It had been so easy. No one would think of looking for him here. Brad was very proud of himself.

He looked down at his watch. It was already 12:30 – lunchtime. He rummaged through his pack and pulled out the bread, mustard, and ham to make two huge sandwiches.

A wren came daringly close to share his last crumbs before Brad reluctantly rose and started along the path again.

His family and his cousin's family had camped at Longford for the past two years. He and his father had often hiked to the hut and stayed overnight. Brad always remembered these times with his father. He remembered, too, the early morning stillness of the forest and how they shared their breakfast cooked over the big, old fireplace in the scruffy – but comfortable – hut.

Brad was now heading to this hut. He had to follow the riverside path until it forked. Then, he had to follow the fork that had the sign about the hut. Brad's only worry was that he needed to reach the hut before dark. He couldn't remember how long it had taken them last time.

Suddenly, Brad stood stock-still. Voices! He could hear voices out here in the wilderness. In one leap, he sprang down the sloping path, slid sideways, and then crouched behind a log.

It was only after the crunch of footsteps and the sound of voices began to fade that Brad dared to raise his head. His rapid heartbeat slowed as he made his way back to the path and saw two men retreating, carrying heavy backpacks. He must be more careful about meeting the occasional hiker. Anyone he met would definitely ask what he was doing out here on his own.

Brad resumed his trek. In less than half an hour, he reached the fork in the path. He found the rough wooden sign for the hut tacked to a tree. The arrow pointed to a path that went up the left side of the river. The path veered uphill and would take longer than the easy riverside walk on the other bank.

Brad was glad to escape most of the sun in the thicker, shadier forest. He wished he could have stopped to take a swim in the cool river now behind him. Perhaps then his back wouldn't feel so hot and sweaty under his backpack.

Brad rested but didn't eat anything. He would save his appetite for the meal he was going to cook in the hut. As he began the sloping climb again, he planned a menu in his mind. His mouth watered.

After that, he thought, he would roll out his sleeping bag in the light of the fire and lie down on one of the bunks.

It was nearly six o'clock when he rounded a bend in the path and saw the hut. Brad smiled in delight. The hut was slightly smaller than he remembered. It was nestled in a ring of towering trees. A water tank leaned up against one side of it. Ferns clustered close.

Then Brad's smile of satisfaction disappeared. His mouth fell open in dismay. There was smoke floating out of the chimney! Someone was staying in his hideout!

CHAPTER FOUR

Whoever was inside the hut might be staring out a window at him. As though silence would help prevent detection, Brad slowly tiptoed backward, his eyes fixed on the hut door.

The door didn't open. Nobody yelled. There was silence except for the sound of his own rapid, shallow breathing. Brad crouched back in the cover of some undergrowth at the edge of the clearing and allowed a soft groan to escape. What was he going to do now?

His stomach unexpectedly rumbled as he thought of the delicious hot meal that he had been looking forward to eating. Tears sprang to his eyes. He dashed them away angrily. What was the point of crying like a little kid?

Brad couldn't even think straight. He just sat there, staring at the hut, hoping for an answer.

Finally, Brad realized that the chimney smoke was decreasing in volume rather than increasing. If people were in there cooking a meal, why were they letting the fire dwindle away?

He sprang to his feet, filled with a sudden inspiration. Maybe the two hikers who passed him earlier were the ones staying there. And maybe the smoke was from the fire they had made to cook their dinner! That could mean there was no one there now!

Then, he sank into hiding again. How was he going to find out for sure? He could throw a stone at the door, and anyone inside would open the door to see who was knocking. He felt the ground around his feet. There weren't any stones, but he found a piece of rotten wood.

Brad hid his backpack beneath a log and climbed up a nearby tree until he was well screened by its leafy branches. Checking his balance, he carefully leaned out, took aim, and hurled the piece of wood as hard as he could.

It shattered with a satisfying crash against the door and flew apart in a shower of splinters. Brad held his breath, his eyes fixed on the door. He waited for a full minute. Nobody came out.

Grinning in relief, but still cautious, Brad slid down the tree. He slipped along the edge of the clearing, then through the trees next to the hut. Silently, he crept up to the small window on the back wall and peered inside.

The window was grimy and dark. Brad could only just make out shadowy outlines. Poised to flee if anyone answered, he tapped sharply on the window and hissed, "Anyone there?" Apart from the beating of his heart and the twittering of a bird, there was silence.

Brad grinned broadly. All that panic and all that waiting was for absolutely nothing. Slipping around to the front of the hut, Brad pushed the door open. For the second time in half an hour, disappointment wiped Brad's smile of satisfaction from his face.

Three sleeping bags had been tossed out onto the bunks, and a heap of dishes and food cluttered the counter. Towels were hung on a piece of twine stretching from wall to wall, and a pile of clothes lay crumpled on the floor.

Brad was seized by fright. Any minute now the hut's occupants could walk in the door. Pulling the door closed behind him, he turned and ran back to his hiding place in the undergrowth.

For the second time, tears sprang to his eyes, and this time he let them trickle down his cheeks. His stomach gurgled. A stick poked painfully into his knee. Brad pushed it aside. A tear splashed on the ground beside his hand.

"Well, at least I'm going to have some food, even if it's not hot." He pulled out his pack to get the rest of the loaf of bread. It couldn't compare with the sweet-and-sour pork he had planned on cooking from a dehydrated food package. But at least it was food, and he was feeling hungry.

Brad found that eating some sardines, bread, and apples made him feel much better.

So there was someone in his hut. OK, he'd find somewhere else to spend the night. The hikers wouldn't be there forever. If he bedded down somewhere, not too far away, he could watch in the morning and see if they left. It had been stupid of him to not have thought of anyone being there. If these people did leave and he was able to take over the hut, he was still going to worry whether anyone else would turn up.

Brad thrust that thought aside for the moment. Right now he had to find somewhere to sleep. Before he shouldered his pack, Brad dragged out a sweater. The chill of the evening was settling in.

He decided to go back into the forest, keeping off the path. He would find a good place to construct some kind of shelter. A shiver crept over him as he thought about sleeping outside.

A hundred or so paces from his starting point, Brad used his pocket knife to cut a mark on the trunk of a large tree. He climbed on, marking a tree here and there. "I bet those hikers are on their way back now, all ready to have a hot dinner," he muttered.

Suddenly, he found he was heading downhill. The undergrowth looked promising, but the ground was slightly damp and he could hear running water. He turned slightly left, keeping to the edge of the basin he had wandered into, and as he climbed over its shoulder, he saw that off to the left was a large fallen tree. He scrambled through ferns and small rotting branches, toward it. If he plucked some big fern leaves and broke off a few rotten branches, he could create a roof by leaning the leaves and branches against the fallen tree.

He worked energetically as the light began to fade. Then he paused, looking to see if he could see smoke rising from the hut's chimney.

But because he was lower than the basin of the forest, the fall of the land obscured the hut. And he was too far away to have the company of the distant voices in the hut.

Brad continued to work on his shelter. It didn't look great, but he would just have to do the best he could. People didn't need him, and he didn't need people. He'd manage by himself. Turtle was going to be really impressed when he told him all about it.

When Brad finally crawled into his shelter and on his bed of ferns, he knew it wouldn't be comfortable, but it was dry and had the effect of walls comfortably enclosing him.

Within minutes, Brad dozed off to sleep.

CHAPTER FIVE

When he awoke to the darkness of the night, Brad felt rising panic. Was this a nightmare? What was the tickling, feathery substance underneath his hands? As his hands recoiled from the ferns, he sat up, hitting his head sharply on the branch above him. The flood of pain mingled with a flood of memory. He was in the forest and alone, completely alone.

What had woken him? Was there something out there, out in the dark, waiting for him? Brad was not cold, but he curled farther down into his sleeping bag. He tried to reassure himself that if he survived the night, he could go home in the morning. Home. He didn't mind which home it was, as long as he was safe within real walls.

Was his mother sleeping now or worrying about him? Tears trickled down Brad's cheeks.

Had she called his father? She'd probably just called Gary Hebbleton.

What was that noise? Just in time, Brad stopped himself from sitting bolt upright. A crawling feeling slid up and down his spine. What animal made a noise like that? Maybe it was some undiscovered animal. A cold sweat broke out all over his body.

A small wind rustling the loose leaves of his shelter seemed like a searching hand that was trying to reach in and grab him. Brad clasped his hands over his head and shrank back as close as possible to the log behind him – as far from the rustling leaves as he could get.

Only after a despairing period of muffled sobbing did Brad sleep again. Twice more he woke to experience the same dreadful fear and terrifying loneliness. The second time, he could see the gray light of dawn filtering into his shelter, and he didn't try to go back to sleep. He lay waiting for the comfort of morning.

It seemed, however, as if morning would never come, and eventually Brad stiffly climbed out of his shelter, as if his wakefulness might help hurry the morning's arrival.

Above him the last stars were fading. The treetops were black against the sky and looked like stenciled patterns he had made at school.

Brad saw the beauty of it all. He allowed his eyes to wander into shadowy corners. There was nothing frightening there, just whispering leaves touched by a rippling breeze. As the light increased, he could see beads of dew gleaming. That slight movement by his foot was a small insect beginning its day's work.

The trees were tall and silent, like sentries that had been on guard all night. The world was again a fresh and beautiful place. A bird sang.

Although his fear and loneliness were not part of this new day, Brad still felt the echoes of them. He dragged out his backpack and sleeping bag and dismantled the shelter, piece by piece.

There was no way he'd spend another night in it. If necessary, he would sneak back to the barbecue facilities at the edge of the forest. There was a walled shelter there that he could creep into for the night.

He washed his face with a handful of dew. There was no one to tell him to brush his hair. For his breakfast, Brad ate the other can of sardines, a slice of bread, and an apple. He wished there was water handy to make himself a drink of fruit juice.

So what if he had been a little scared in the night? So what if his mother was worried? So what if his father didn't even know where he was? He was OK on his own. Brad leaned his backpack against the trunk of a large tree and planned his next move. "I'll just go over that rise and see if there are still people in my hut."

CHAPTER SIX

The sun sent long, gold fingers through the tall trees. A distant water sound trickled musically between snatches of birdsong. What a morning to be walking through the forest!

Brad had marked some trees yesterday. Now, when he thought he was retracing his steps, he couldn't find one of the crosses anywhere. Every moss-covered trunk seemed untouched. He took ten paces left and looked again. Nothing. He moved ten paces forward. Nothing. He moved right and twenty paces back. Brad's heart beat a little faster.

"I won't panic," he told himself. "I didn't stay very far from that hut. Where was my shelter? I'll find it and start again."

The shelter was nowhere in sight. Brad circled a large area and saw nothing that remotely resembled it, and nothing that looked like the hut. A sudden swish made him jump. It was a forest bird swooping overhead.

"I know – I'll climb a tree! I should have thought of that before."

Many of the trees had long, smooth trunks with branches that were out of reach. Then, he came upon one tree with a rotting trunk leaning against it. He scrambled up and was just able to swing himself onto a lower branch. "I'm saving the view for the end," he panted at a darting bird as he hauled himself up, higher and higher. He stopped when the branches started to become slender again. Now he'd find out where he was.

But he didn't. A thousand other trees, maybe even a million, were surrounding him, he decided angrily. His view was only the high, leafy branches. To his left, the ground dropped, and all he could see was an aerial view of treetops. But he couldn't see anything else.

There was no smoke marking the hut chimney, or a glimpse anywhere of faded, red paint. Just leaves and branches and treetops all around.

Brad scrambled down the tree and sat on the leafy carpet at its foot to think. His mouth felt strangely dry.

Again he decided to mark the tree with his knife, to ensure that he didn't start going around in circles. Then, he realized that he didn't have his knife. He had put it in his pack, which was propped beneath a tree. Which tree? He couldn't find the tree. He had no idea where to start looking for it.

Brad leaped to his feet. If he couldn't find his pack, he had no extra clothes and no food. He shouldn't have left it, not even for a moment. "I don't need a knife, though. I can break branches."

With no idea of which direction he was heading, Brad started forward, his feet moving as fast as his racing heart. Every few paces, he reached up to eye level and snapped a small branch, leaving it dangling like a broken wing, as an obvious marker.

It must have been half an hour before his eyes, which were darting from side to side in a desperate search for a familiar landmark, stopped darting and fixed, horror-struck, on a small broken branch.

He was going around in circles! No hut, no pack, and walking in circles. He didn't start to cry. He was too shocked. He stood, staring at the branch as though he might make it disappear, and remove this awful proof of his inability to walk in a straight line. But it hung there limply. A stray puff of morning breeze swung it to and fro for a moment. Brad reached out suddenly and, with one swipe, knocked it to the ground. Then, he whirled around and started to run. He must find his pack. He must find the hut. He must find where he was.

His feet flashed through ferns, over logs, through soggy hollows of brown mud, around trees, and over fallen branches. He went up a rise and down a hollow. Sticks crackled under his feet; branches clawed at his clothes; startled birds fluttered to escape him. He ran until his breath rasped in his chest and burned like fire under his ribs. He ran until his legs felt like shaking jelly.

Then, when he could run no more, Brad threw himself down in a clump of ferns and sobbed. Gradually, his sobbing reduced itself to a soft sniffling. The pain in his chest subsided. His legs stopped shaking. Brad got to his hands and knees, and then to his feet. The only thought in his mind was that he must keep going. He was no longer sure why.

He stared through eyes still blurry from his tears. His feet stumbled over roots and sticks and clumps of undergrowth. Clunk, clunk, stumble, clunk. He kept going, even though his feet and his hands hardly seemed to belong to him anymore. Clunk, stumble, clunk, clunk.

Then, all at once, he was falling! He flailed and kicked through a tangle of ferns and branches. He bounced against a bank, feeling a sting of pain as a branch whipped his face and a jarring jolt as his back hit a rock. In a tangle of branches, he hit the ground at the bottom of the cliff he had gone over, his face slapping hard into a pile of damp leaves.

For a minute he didn't dare move in case he was badly injured. Gingerly, he pulled up one leg and then the other. They were OK. He lifted his face and watched a drop of blood splatter from his cheek onto the ground. He carefully turned his head right, then left. His neck wasn't broken. He pushed himself into a sitting position. Relieved that his limbs were functioning, he let himself roll back. His back hurt from his fall, and he slowly rolled to one side.

Then he saw it! There, right beside his face, poking out from a clump of ferns, was a hand! A human hand!

For one startled second, Brad thought it might be his. A quick glance assured him that both of his hands were still attached. He scrambled to his feet. With horrified eyes fixed on the hand, Brad took several steps backward and tripped. Had another hand tripped him? He lay there for a moment and then, slowly, slowly, turned his head to look at the hand. It moved! Brad let out a shriek of pure fright and leaped to his feet again.

CHAPTER SEVEN

The hand groped and reached forward. Brad saw an arm emerging from the ferns and branches. A man's head lifted out of the foliage. His eyes registered Brad's presence.

Brad swallowed to moisten his mouth. He ran a hand over his head (for he was sure his hair was standing on end with fright) and let a fluttering sigh of relief escape. Thank goodness the hand actually belonged to a live body.

Brad took a cautious step forward. There was another groan, a mutter, and the owner of the hand tottered to his feet. Almost immediately, the tall man sat down again, cradling his bleeding hand against his chest.

Brad wasn't good at guessing ages. The man looked like he was in good shape, and his face showed some lines. The dark hair had flecks of gray. As Brad stared, the brown face seemed to grow pale. The man groaned again and muttered something.

Then he grinned feebly. "It's the sight of my own blood. Do you have anything I could put around my hand?"

For a moment, Brad stood helpless. Then he pulled from his pocket a large handkerchief that used to belong to his dad. "Here, take this." He offered the handkerchief. "It's pretty clean."

The man wrapped it clumsily over his bleeding hand. Brad wished he knew more about first aid.

"Where's your father?" The question took Brad by surprise.

"At home." That wasn't really lying, Brad decided. He might be at his home.

There was a short silence. "Who are you with?"

"No one," Brad said.

"Are you on your own?" The man was startled.

"Yep."

"How old are you?"

"Eleven."

"Don't you go to school?"

"Yep."

"Well, what are you doing in the middle of the forest all by yourself?"

Brad stared back and answered with some defiance. "I ran away."

"I see." The man stared at him for a moment.

Brad shuffled his feet uncomfortably in the fallen leaves. Was it only yesterday that he'd been at home? Was it only yesterday that he'd climbed off the bus and wandered happily along the first forest path, feeling as though he were king of the world? Yesterday seemed so far back in time. Today he was lost, and he wasn't going to tell this inquisitive man that.

"Anyway, why are you here? What happened to you?" Brad asked.

"I fell down that stupid cliff." The color had returned to the man's face, and with his good hand he was brushing the leaves out of his hair while he held his hurt hand close to his chest. "What a dumb thing to do. I heard something tearing through the forest, and I turned around to look. I must have kept walking backward and pow! I went over." A thought seemed to strike him. "Were you the one making all that noise?" The man was piecing things together.

"It could have been me." There seemed no sense in denying it. "I'm not that good at going quietly in the forest," Brad added.

"You could say that again," the man said dryly. "My name is Barrett, Dave Barrett. What's yours?"

Brad told him.

"Well, I seem to be practically in one piece," said Dave. "How about you? It seems to me you shot over the side, too. You all right? Something cut your face a little."

Brad had forgotten. He touched the clotting blood on his scratched cheek. "It's OK. I bruised my back, but it'll be all right."

"Ahhh." Dave winced as he tried to stand up.

"My ankle is definitely messed up. Give me a hand to find my pack, Brad."

They searched at the base of the low cliff until Brad spotted the pack up in some branches.

"I'll let that be your job," said Dave.

Brad scrambled up. "Give it a push and let it roll down," called Dave.

Half an hour later, they had Dave's camp stove burning merrily. They ate cabin bread with cheese, and were waiting for a cup of coffee. Brad really didn't like drinking coffee, but here in the forest, he thought coffee might taste OK.

Dave really knew how to manage. To keep it from swelling any more, he'd wrapped his ankle in a T-shirt that he had soaked in the nearby stream. The ankle wasn't broken, he told Brad after feeling it carefully and expertly. It was just sprained. Brad had to help get things out of Dave's pack because Dave's hand was still wrapped in Brad's handkerchief.

"I'll look at it later," he told Brad.

The sun, now high in the sky, poured into the clearing by the stream. The water in the pot began to bubble gently, and the stream gurgled a happy sound between mossy banks. A wren hopped close to Brad. Brad smiled to himself. "Boy, will Turtle be mad that he isn't here with me," he thought.

When Dave unwound the handkerchief from his hand, he and Brad saw that a jagged piece of flesh was ripped back, leaving half of the palm raw and meaty.

"I'm not too thrilled about the sight of my own blood," said Dave.

Brad didn't like the sight much himself. "You should clean it, shouldn't you?"

Using the warm water still left in the pot, Brad helped Dave wash the hand clean and pat it dry with a worn towel. While Dave clenched his teeth, Brad lifted the flap of skin back into position, and they taped it down using three Band-Aids Brad found in the side pocket of Dave's pack.

Dave held the cuff of a spare shirt in his good hand while Brad hacked the sleeve off with Dave's knife. They wrapped the sleeve around Dave's hand and pulled a sock that should have been cleaner over the top like a mitten. Dave seemed glad to have his injury out of sight.

"Thanks, kid." He feigned a couple of gentle boxing blows with his gloved hand. "It'll be like new before you know it." But Brad noticed he cradled it carefully.

Brad splashed his own face in the stream, pretending it didn't feel sore at all, in spite of the stinging scratches.

"Look at this ankle," Dave said, probing it gently as Brad soaked the T-shirt in water again. "It doesn't look too bad. We'll camp here tonight. There's time enough for walking in the morning."

CHAPTER EIGHT

Dave lay back on the bank of the stream. "I think we deserve a little time for forty winks."

Brad found he was more comfortable sitting than lying on his back. Why did adults waste daytime sleeping?

"Are you camped near here somewhere?" Dave said suddenly.

"Ummm... yes." Brad glanced sideways. Dave was staring straight at him. "I thought I might stay here tonight," Brad said hastily. "Make sure you're OK and all that."

"Oh, yeah?" Dave's eyes kept boring into his.

Brad got to his feet and kicked a few sticks. "Would you like me to?" he asked tentatively.

"Fine with me," Dave said. "Do you have your own sleeping bag?"

"It's in my pack."

Brad didn't want to admit to this "expert" that he'd done something as stupid as losing his pack. He glanced at Dave's dirt-stained, well-used pack. Dave would never have let his backpack out of his sight.

Brad wondered if he could say that his camp was too far away to go and get a sleeping bag. He decided to change the subject until he had had time to think about it. "Do you come into the forest often?"

Dave's eyes carefully studied Brad for a moment longer. Then the lids half-dropped, and relaxed. "Quite a bit."

"Tell me more," Brad said quickly.

During the next hour, Brad learned a lot about living in the forest. If Dave noticed that Brad's questions were coming thick and fast to keep the conversation away from him, he didn't let on.

"I used to hike a lot more," Dave finished. "These days, I only get back to the forest now and again, and then it's just for a few days.

I thought maybe elephants had moved in when I heard you this morning."

Brad, startled, turned slightly red. "I was in kind of a hurry."

"I never thought that running away actually meant that you had to run all the time." There was a pause. "What made you run away in the first place?"

Brad didn't say anything. Without looking up, he could feel Dave's eyes boring into him again. Even when he turned his head to one side it was as if they bored through the back of his head.

"Don't you like your parents?"

"Of course I do."

"Are they mean to you?"

"No," Brad said, glaring at Dave and then looking away.

Dave left the silence hanging for a while. Brad groped in his mind for the right thing to say.

"Well, if your parents treat you OK, then what's the big problem? Don't you like school?"

How could Brad explain his feelings to this man when he couldn't even explain them to Turtle? How could he explain how his problems kept piling on top of one another?

"Well?"

When Brad glanced up, he saw Dave gazing somewhere into the distance. Brad swallowed quickly and managed to say, "Mom won't buy me a mountain bike."

Dave's head turned slowly. His eyes stared straight at Brad. "Say that again." The voice was soft. Perhaps, Brad decided, he just hadn't heard.

"Mom won't buy me a mountain bike."

"So you ran away?" Dave's voice was still soft, almost as if, Brad thought, he was holding it in.

He answered with some defiance. "Yes, I did."

"I don't believe it." Brad became aware of an expression of scorn on Dave's face.

"Well, she should have bought me a mountain bike. I'm old enough to have one." Brad was starting to believe that not having a bike really was his reason for running away. "And I'm showing her I'm old enough to look after myself..." He was going to say "in the forest," but the memory of his fear last night, his lost pack this morning, and the possibility of being alone again that night, made him stop.

"What on earth makes you think that you should get what you want, when you want it?"

Brad felt anger boiling inside him. He'd dared to think he'd found a friend, but Dave was just another adult after all.

"You know what I think, kid? I think you're a spoiled brat, and if you were mine, I'd ground you for months."

"Well, I'm not your kid! And you can't punish me!" Brad yelled.

Dave looked unimpressed by the anger. Then he gave Brad a half-smile. "Actually, I'm pretty sure you're not telling me the whole story. But I'll tell you this, you've discovered you aren't as grown-up as you thought you were, haven't you?

Are you lost? You were running back there this morning in a wild panic because you didn't know where you were. Right?"

"I was not!" Brad yelled. "I was not!"

"You don't have a camp, do you?" goaded Dave. "You don't have any gear with you. You're a crazy little kid coming out here with nothing."

"I've got a pack! With clothes and food!"

"Where is it, Brad?" Dave asked.

"Never mind!" The pitch of Brad's voice rose again. "And you can take care of yourself tonight for all I care! Make your own stupid cups of coffee. I'm going back to my camp." He turned and started running, and he didn't care that he had no idea where he was heading.

"Brad!" Dave's voice snapped his name out with such authority that Brad's feet stopped moving. "Don't you take one more step. Now turn yourself around and come back here. For now, I'm all you've got."

Brad turned slowly and stared at Dave.

"You're not my father," Brad mumbled, brushing a hand across his face as tears started welling up in his eyes.

"You're lucky I'm not," Dave said grimly. "But I'm a decent person, and I care if you get lost. Do you understand that? I care, and there's no way you're wandering off on your own."

The tears that had started in anger now poured down Brad's face. His voice still raged, but somewhere deep inside him, confusion wove in and out of his anger. "Why should you care? My father doesn't care and my mother doesn't care, so I don't see why you should. Turtle's the only one who cares."

Dave was staring at him.

Brad spoke in a calm voice this time. "I don't care if I have a mountain bike or not," he said. "I don't care one bit, not really. I'm going to get some more water," he added lamely, "in case you want coffee."

"OK," Dave said in a puzzled voice. "Thanks."

CHAPTER NINE

When Brad brought the water back, Dave lit the stove again. They waited in silence for the pot to boil. Eventually, Dave looked at Brad over a steaming cup of coffee. "Will you mind sleeping under the stars?" he asked.

Brad remembered how beautiful the sky had looked in the early morning. "I don't mind. I'd like it."

"Where did you sleep last night?"

"I made a shelter." Brad picked at a clump of moss that looked like a miniature grove of feathery trees. "There was already someone in the hut – that hut at the end of the path coming in."

"I see," said Dave. "Did you sleep well?" His eyes twinkled.

Brad blushed. "Not very well," he mumbled. "I hardly slept at all!"

Suddenly, Brad found himself telling Dave how upset he'd been to discover someone in "his" hut, how he'd wandered far from it, trying to find a place for his shelter, how terrifying waking up at night had been, and how relieved he'd been when morning came. Then, he started talking about the awful despair of discovering he was lost, and finding he'd lost his pack, too. The recollection of that fear still made the edges of his stomach flutter. When he told Dave about the pure terror he'd felt falling into nothingness, and landing only to see a human hand, Dave gave a hearty roar of laughter.

"Not that easy being a forest expert, is it?" Dave said.

"I wish Turtle was with me."

"Who's this Turtle you keep talking about?"

"His real name is George, but once during a track meet, this kid from another school was watching him run way up in front of the other kids. And he said, 'Man, is that one a slow turtle!'

He meant he was really fast," Brad explained, in case Dave didn't get the point. "So now all his friends call him Turtle."

"What makes you think he cares more than your own mother and father?"

"He does. I just know he does." Brad pulled apart another moss clump, searching his mind for a way to explain it to Dave and to himself. "Well, I always know what he's going to do. He doesn't do anything I don't expect!"

Dave frowned and looked bewildered.

"Well, you know, he stays the same. I know where I am. He doesn't change," Brad said.

"You mean your father changes into a frog now and then, and you feel surprised about it." Dave was laughing at him, but not unkindly.

"My father moved away. I haven't seen him for nearly a year," Brad said.

Brad then told Dave how running away was the first thing in ages that he could concentrate on enough to banish the awful things.

"Running away doesn't seem like a very useful thing to concentrate on," Dave eventually said. He picked up a stick, balanced it on his knee with his sore hand, and began whittling at it with his pocketknife held in the other hand. Brad watched for a while.

"I didn't know what else to do," he said at last. Brad told Dave how he'd always used the trick of concentrating on something else to forget the problems that were hurting him. "But nothing worked this time until I thought about running away. I loved my dad. And now he just writes me letters, and I'll never see him again."

"Does he write often?"

"Every week. And he says he's coming home sometime this summer so we can take a trip together. I don't believe him. If you go away without saying good-bye, well, you're not going to bother coming back, are you?"

Brad told Dave about Gary Hebbleton and how his mom would probably run off with him.

He said he knew Gary Hebbleton wouldn't want him. Brad went on to explain how their house was being sold and that someone else was going to live in it and that his mother wanted to buy another house, which he knew would be terrible.

"My mother said I could have my room any way I liked, and then she said I couldn't paint it black. I won't be able to have my room the way I want it at all."

When he finally stopped talking, Brad felt as though he had let a large pile of problems spill out of his head. There was room for his brain to think again. He should have told Turtle everything a long time ago.

"You should run for office in the government. The president could use someone just like you." Dave was whittling his stick and not looking up at Brad.

Brad stared at him. "What do you mean?"

"Well, it would be really helpful for the president to always know what everybody thought. The president could say, 'Brad, you can read minds. What do people think about this?'"

"That's stupid," Brad muttered.

"Well, you seem sure you know what your mother and father and everyone else thinks."

"You think I'm lying to you?"

"Not lying, exactly. You're just making all these assumptions."

"What does assumptions mean?" Brad asked.

"Assuming. Thinking you know but not having anything to prove it."

"My father did leave us. I'm not lying."

"Look, I believe you, Brad. But you said that your dad's not coming back. You are assuming that he isn't. It seems like a pretty strange assumption to me, when he said he's coming to visit during his vacation. I mean, he can hardly visit every weekend if he lives far away, can he? Seems to me he's doing really well writing to you every week. Every week's pretty good."

"Do you really think so?" asked Brad.

"Well, do you write him a letter every week?"

Brad blushed. "No, not every week."

"I bet you don't. But your father just keeps on writing, even if you don't write back. It seems to me he's the kind of guy who's going to come over and see you when he says he will," Dave said.

"Do you really think so?"

"I do. And what about this Hebbleton guy? Why do you think your mother would run off with him? Did she say she was going to?"

"No," Brad said.

"Has she been going out with him a lot?"

Brad hesitated. "Not really."

"How often?"

"Once." Brad's voice was small.

Dave was pointing a finger at him, laughing. "Once! Once! You don't run off with someone when you've gone out with them once! Why would she be buying a house if she was leaving? Now, she's looked after you for your whole life. Why would she give up on you now?"

There was silence for a while. Brad couldn't think of anything to say.

"And another thing," said Dave, "if you were my kid and wanted to paint your room black, I wouldn't let you, either. What a silly idea! But it wouldn't mean you couldn't paint it just about any other color."

Dave folded his pocketknife and got to his feet. He shook the whittled stick at Brad. "Things change. People change. It's no use running away. That won't change things back.

"Now, I don't have two good hands, and you don't have a sleeping bag. We need to make a sleeping place for the night, so we better join forces. At first light tomorrow we're heading out of here, ankle or no ankle, and getting you home where you belong."

As Brad got to his feet, Dave stepped toward him. His eyes softened, and he spoke quietly. "Look, I'm not pretending it doesn't hurt, kid. I know it hurts. My mother left our house when I was eight. There were no letters – nothing. I've never seen her to this day."

There was silence – a silence filled with the sharpness of Dave's recalled pain. In it, for the first time ever, Brad felt an adult's pain. It hurt almost as much as if it were his own.

Then Dave turned, burrowed in his pack, and brought out a large hunting knife. "Well, come on," he briskly said to Brad. "Come on, and no more nonsense about people not caring. Right?"

Brad fell into step behind Dave as he headed across the clearing and into the forest.

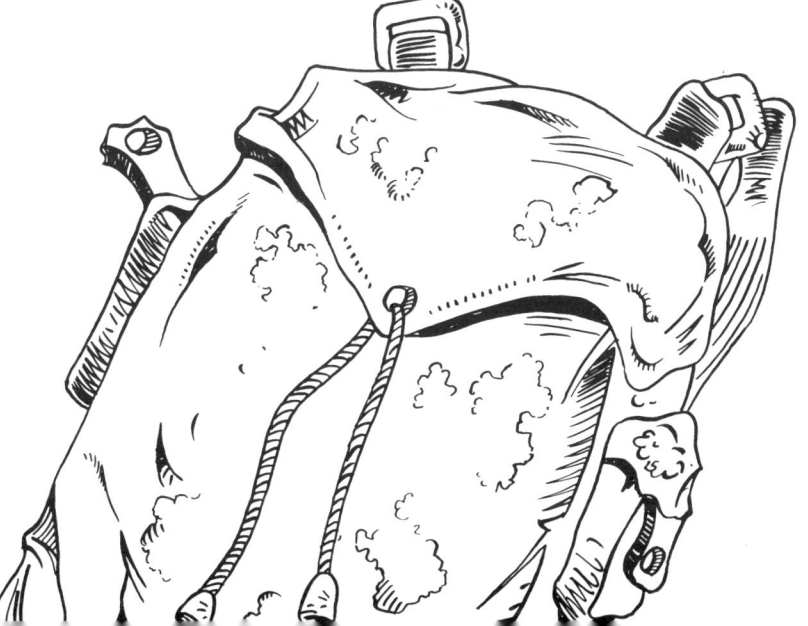

CHAPTER TEN

Dave used his knife to cut a pile of young, leafy branches. He and Brad carried them back to the clearing. Dave soaked his ankle again in cold water, declaring that the swelling had gone down and the pain was less, although he still limped.

The summer sun was still shining even though the day was nearly at its end as they lit the camp stove and put on a pot of water to boil. Dave threw in a handful of rice and then the contents of a dehydrated food package. Soon, delicious smells rose over the smoke of the fire. Brad's stomach rumbled in anticipation. Finally, when the meal was ready, he ate his share from Dave's plate and Dave ate straight from the pot. Food had never tasted so good. After their meal, Dave made himself some coffee, and they both ate cabin bread and cheese.

Later, Dave showed Brad how to construct a low shelter over a large groundsheet that he spread on the ground over some of the springiest branches. Sometimes, as they worked, Dave and Brad talked. Sometimes they were silent. They didn't speak again about Brad's problems or of his disasters in the forest. They chatted instead about camping, about favorite TV programs, and about what sort of car each would buy if they were millionaires. Brad told Dave about school, and Dave told him about his work with a transportation company.

In the back of Brad's mind, he again had space for positive thoughts. And now he would always know that sharing problems made them hurt less.

As the dusk deepened, Dave crawled into his sleeping bag. Brad put on two of Dave's thick wool sweaters and tucked his feet snugly into Dave's backpack. Brad felt surprisingly warm and comfortable.

He had planned to watch the sky until the first few stars above him had multiplied into millions more. But his eyelids closed and he slept a deep and untroubled sleep until morning.

After cleaning up their campsite, Brad and Dave started out to find the hut.

"Do you really know the way?" It seemed to Brad that the first half hour of walking wasn't getting them anywhere.

"Well, let's say I have a much better idea than you do," returned Dave.

Dave's ankle slowed him down but, even so, Brad was just able to keep up with him as they made their way through ferns and the new growth of regenerating forest. Then there was a path to follow, not human-made, but obvious enough to make walking simpler and to allow Brad enough breath to talk.

"Hey, Dave, are you married?" Brad hurriedly asked between breaths.

"No. Not yet."

"Not yet! How old are you?" Right away he felt glad he was behind Dave so that he couldn't be seen turning red. Adults didn't always like being asked how old they were.

Dave gave a great burst of laughter. "You think I'm too old? I'm only thirty-one. And I have a female friend who thinks that's just right."

Brad didn't know what to say, so he said nothing. So Dave had a girlfriend... Thirty-one seemed pretty old, actually.

Three-quarters of an hour later, Dave stopped and pointed. "See that?"

Brad craned forward. There was a small patch of red between some trees. "We're at the hut!"

"We'll be home in no time," said Dave.

A peculiar feeling welled up in the bottom of Brad's stomach. Home. Feelings flashed in confused order – guilt, defiance, shame. Every few seconds, his stomach seemed to suddenly turn over, as if his breakfast were practicing somersaults. Dave's voice echoed in his mind.

"Things change. People change. It's no use running away," he'd said.

The men who had been in the hut were gone. When Dave said he'd like to rest there for fifteen minutes, Brad felt glad to have one last delay before they finally walked out. He sat on a bunk and wondered what he would have been doing now if this hut had been empty when he walked into the forest two days ago. Two days ago – it seemed more like a lifetime.

He felt Dave's eyes on him. "Do you think your mother might let you come out on a hike with me some time? Would you like to?" Dave asked.

Brad's stomach turned another somersault at being reminded of how soon he must face his mother. At the same time, he felt both surprised and happy. "Would you really? Would you really take me out on a hike?"

"Your mother might let you come some time – if you get your act together and let her see you're starting to grow up a little."

Brad couldn't sit still. Crossing to the hut doorway, he looked up the path that would lead them back to Longford and then to home. He was surprised to see two figures in the distance, a boy and a man. Even from this distance, Brad could tell the boy was about his size. He was wearing a red-and-black T-shirt just like the one Turtle's father had bought for Turtle. Brad turned to tell Dave that someone was coming.

Then he whirled around to look at them again. "It is!" He dived inside the doorway and said, "It's Turtle! What's he doing here? I told him not to tell!"

"What?"

Brad looked out the door again. "It's Turtle! He's got someone with him. I told Turtle not to tell."

Dave was beside him now, looking out the door. "I trusted him," Brad groaned.

"Now, wait a minute, I thought you said he cared about you," said Dave.

"That's what I thought!" Thinking Dave was agreeing with him, Brad repeated it with more emphasis. "That's what I thought!"

"Well, you're right," said Dave. "He cared enough to come and look for you." Brad felt a second of betrayal and was about to protest until Dave continued. "If I hadn't been out there for you to trip over and you were still lost – and you *were* lost – you'd be glad Turtle cared enough to bring someone to look for you," he said.

Brad was quiet. He'd asked his friend not to tell. But was Dave right? Was it because Turtle cared that he had told someone? What if he had still been lost out there in the forest?

There was another man coming now, a short distance behind Turtle and his companion. Brad would have known that hat anywhere. It was Mr. Taylor, Turtle's father.

Well, who was the man with Turtle? Who was it? He banged a fist suddenly on the open door of the hut.

"It's him!" he told Dave. "It's Gary Hebbleton."

Dave put a hand on Brad's shoulder. "You know that job I thought you could get with the president? Well, forget it – I don't think you could do it, when I think about it."

Turtle and Gary Hebbleton could see them now. Turtle was waving, and his face was one wide smile of delight. Brad waved back, but his eyes were firmly on Dave.

"What on earth are you talking about now?" he demanded.

"Your mind-reading abilities – they're all wrong." He gestured toward the approaching pair. "You assumed this man didn't like you. I don't think Gary Hebbleton would be here if he didn't think you were worth finding."

Brad made a small, defiant frown. "It's because of my mom. It's probably because he likes her."

Just then, Gary Hebbleton's face broke into a smile. Not even Brad could deny the warmth in it. "Brad! Am I glad to see you! I told your mother you'd be all right. But all the same, I'm really glad to see you!"

Dave hissed into Brad's ear, "You definitely couldn't get a job with the president."

"Hello, Gary," said Brad. "Hi, Turtle. It's good to see you." He glanced from one to the other. "Good to see you both."

FROM THE AUTHOR

Many years ago, I discovered that characters in books laughed and cried, hurt and healed, the same way we do in real life. I discovered that reading about their life journeys helps me cope with my own.

I like to write stories about the tunnels that some of us have to crawl through on our journeys. Maybe Brad's tunnel is one you know about. Maybe it isn't, but "being there" with Brad might help you understand what being in that tunnel feels like.

Whether you identify with Brad's experience or not, I hope you enjoy being part of it. A good read is like time spent with a good friend!

Pauline Cartwright

FROM THE ILLUSTRATOR

WHEN THINGS GO WRONG
The Long Walk Home
The Trouble with Patrick
The Kids from Quiller's Bend
Laughter Is the Best Medicine
Wild Horses
The Sunday Horse

SOMETHING STRANGE
My Father the Mad Professor
A Theft in Time: Timedetectors II
CD and the Giant Cat
Chocolate!
White Elephants and Yellow Jackets
Dream Boat

ANOTHER TIME, ANOTHER PLACE
Cloudcatcher
Flags
The Dinosaur Connection
Myth or Mystery?
Where Did the Maya Go?
The Journal: Dear Future II

CONFIDENCE AND COURAGE
Imagine This, James Robert
Follow That Spy!
Who Will Look Out for Danny?
Fuzz and the Glass Eye
Bald Eagles
Cottle Street

Written by **Pauline Cartwright**
Illustrated by **Paul Rogers**
Edited by **Ann-Marie Heffernan**
Designed by **Kristie Rogers**

© 1997 Shortland Publications
All rights reserved.

07 06 05 04 03 02
11 10 9 8 7 6 5 4

Distributed in the United States of America by
  Rigby
  a division of Reed Elsevier Inc.
  1000 Hart Road
  Barrington, 60010-2627

Printed in China through Colorcraft Ltd., Hong Kong
ISBN: 0-7901-1694-4